Furniture From Baroque to Rococo

The 18th Century in European Furniture Design

By

Peter Philp

Copyright © 2011 Read Books Ltd.
This book is copyright and may not be
reproduced or copied in any way without
the express permission of the publisher in writing

British Library Cataloguing-in-Publication Data
A catalogue record for this book is available from
the British Library

A History of Furniture

Furniture is the mass noun for the movable objects intended to support various human activities, such as seating, storing, working and sleeping. Most often, at least in the present day - furniture is the product of a lengthy design process and considered a form of decorative art. In addition to furniture's functional role, it can also serve a symbolic or religious purpose, for instance in churches, temples or shrines. It can be made from many materials, including metal, plastic, and wood - using a variety of techniques, joins and decoration, reflecting the local culture from which it originated.

Furniture has been a part of the human experience since the development of non-nomadic cultures, and even before this in its crudest form. Evidence of furniture survives from the Neolithic Period and later in antiquity in the form of paintings, such as the wall Murals discovered at Pompeii; sculpture, and examples have been excavated in Egypt and found in tombs in Ghiordes, in modern-day Turkey. Perhaps one of the most interesting archaeological sites is Skara Brae, a Neolithic village located in Orkney (an archipelago in northern Scotland). The site dates from 3100–2500 BC and due to a shortage of wood in Orkney, the people of Skara Brae were forced to build with stone, a readily available material that could be worked easily and turned into household items. Each house shows a high degree of sophistication and was equipped with an extensive assortment of stone furniture, ranging from cupboards, dressers and beds to shelves, stone seats, and limpet tanks. The stone dresser was regarded as the most important item, as it symbolically faced the entrance in each house and was therefore the first item seen when entering.

The furniture of the Middle Ages was usually heavy, oak, and ornamented with carved designs. Along with the other arts, the Italian Renaissance of the fourteenth and fifteenth century marked a rebirth in design, often inspired by the Greco-Roman tradition. A similar explosion of design, and renaissance of culture in general, occurred in Northern Europe, starting in the fifteenth century. The seventeenth century, in both Southern and Northern Europe, was characterized by opulent, often gilded Baroque designs that frequently incorporated a profusion of vegetal and scrolling ornament. Starting in the eighteenth century, furniture designs began to develop more rapidly. Although there were some styles that belonged primarily to one nation, such as 'Palladianism' in Great Britain (derived from and inspired by the designs of the Venetian architect Andrea Palladio) or 'Louis Quinze' in French furniture (characterised by supreme craftsmanship and the integration of the arts of cabinet-making, painting, and sculpture), others, such as 'Rococo' and 'Neoclassicism' were perpetuated throughout Western Europe.

The nineteenth century is usually defined by concurrent revival styles, including Gothic, Neoclassicism, and Roccoco. The design reforms of the late century introduced the 'Aesthetic movement' (essentially promoting the beauty of objects above any other social or political themes) and the 'Arts and Crafts movement' (An international design movement that flourished between 1860-1910, led by William Morris. It stood for traditional craftsmanship using simple form, often applying medieval, romantic or folk styles of decoration). Art Nouveau, in turn was influenced by both of these movements. This latter development was perhaps the most influential of all, inspired by natural forms and structures; evident primarily in architecture, but also the beautiful objects crafted to fill such spaces. Noted furniture designers in this style included William H. Bradley; the 'Dean of American Designers', Goerges de Feure, the Parisian designer who famously produced the theatre designs for *Le Chat Noir* cabaret, and Hermann Obrist, a German sculptor of the Jugendstil (the German branch of Art Nouveaux) movement.

The first three-quarters of the twentieth century are often seen as the march towards Modernism in furniture design. Modernism, in general, includes the activities and creations of those who felt traditional forms of art, architecture, literature, religious faith and social activities were becoming outdated in the new economic, social, and political environment of an emergent industrialized world. Art Deco, De Stijl, Bauhaus, Wiener Werkstätte, and Vienna Secession designers all worked to some degree within the Modernist idiom. Born from the Bauhaus and Art Deco/Streamline styles came the post WWII 'Mid-Century Modern' style using materials developed during the war including laminated plywood, plastics and fibreglass. Prime examples include furniture designed by George Nelson Associates, Charles and Ray Eames, Paul McCobb and Danish modern designers including Finn Juhl and Arne Jacobsen. Post-modern design, intersecting the Pop art movement, gained steam in the 1960s and 70s, promoted in the 1980s by groups such as the Italy-based Memphis movement. The latter group worked with ephemeral designs, featuring colourful decoration and asymmetrical shapes.

As is evident from this short history, the history of artistic developments is inextricably linked with the progression of furniture design. This is hardly surprising, as after all, many artists, thinkers and designers would stringently resist any artificial separation between traditional fine art and functional design. Both respond to their wider context and environment, both, perhaps in differing ways, seeking to impact on reality and society.

Today, British professional furniture makers have self organised into a strong and vibrant community, largely under the organisation 'The Worshipful Company of Furniture Makers', commonly referred to as the Furniture Makers or the Furniture Makers Company. Its motto is 'Straight and Strong'! Members of the Company come from many professions and disciplines, but the common link is that all members on joining must be engaged in or with the UK furnishing industry. Thus the work of the Company is delivered by members with wide ranging professional knowledge and skills in manufacturing, retailing, education, journalism; in fact any aspect of the industry. There are many similar organisations across the globe, as well as in the UK, all seeking to integrate and promote the valuable art that is furniture making. Education is a key factor in such endeavours, and maintaining strong links between professional practitioners, didactic colleges and the amateur maker/restorer is crucial. We hope the reader enjoys this book.

Contents

	Page No.
France	1
Italy	21
Spain	21
Germany and Sweden	22
The Netherlands	23
Britain	26
America (Colonial Period)	40

Baroque to Rococo

JUST because a new century dawns, it does not necessarily mean that designers rise at the crack of that dawn, bursting with a set of brand new ideas. The eighteenth century is rightly spoken of as the Golden Age of furniture-making, but it must be doubted whether, on 1st January, 1700, the craftsmen of Europe all made good resolutions to devise new forms of unsurpassed elegance.

France

The Régence. At that date, France was still under the political and artistic dictatorship of Louis XIV, and there was little departure from the monumental conception of design until about 1715, when the old devil died. With the possible exception of Madame de Maintenon, everyone was delighted. The king's ambition had brought the country to a state of near-ruin, its extended frontiers a constant temptation to the enemies of France.

Successor to the throne was Louis XV, great-grandson of the old king, but as he was still a minor, his uncle Philip, Duke of Orleans, was accorded the task of ruling the country as regent. Philip's power was, in fact, very limited, and his regency, which lasted for eight years, proved to be a series of well-meant blunders. Our interest in this short epoch of French history is centred on the reaction in taste against the heaviness of the Versailles style under Louis XIV—a reaction which led to a major change in furniture-design throughout Europe.

Its leader was Philip's cabinet-maker, Charles Cressent, who may be said to have created the style we call *Régence*—and if no one minds, we will continue to spell it in the French way, to avoid confusion with the English Regency of a century later.

The most important single aspect of Cressent's work was the switch from rectilinear to curvilinear shapes—not only for legs and other appendages, but also for the actual carcases of many articles. He developed the *bombé commode*, a low chest-of-drawers the front and ends of which swell in serpentine curves longitudinally as well as latitudinally (see Fig. 15). *Bombé*

Fig. 15

The Louis XV Period
Early- to mid-eighteenth century French styles, generally following a sinuous line.
A. *Bombé* commode with ormolu mounts.
B. *Bergère*—cushioned arm-chair.
C. *Secrétaire* with fall-front and *chinoiserie* marquetry decoration.
D. *Bureau-plat*—flat-topped writing-table.

means, simply, 'swollen', and I have heard pieces of this type described, coarsely but vividly, as 'pregnant'. When found in its more extreme form, the shape can be just a little bit repulsive, like some of Ruben's more obese subjects; but when restraint has been employed to impart no more than a gentle swell, the result is as pleasing as the sweetly rounded tums of Botticelli's women.

Cressent was also responsible for a greatly extended use of ormolu mounts (see p. 86), so that they became an integral part of the piece, and not mere applied cornerpieces whose first function had been to protect an edge or corner of Boulle-work (see p. 45). Brass-and-tortoiseshell inlay was now largely abandoned in favour of fine marquetry work in a rich variety of woods.

Though not the creator of the Rococo, Cressent cleared the ground and laid the foundations for it in a way that effectively bridged the gap between the style of Louis XIV and that of Louis XV which was about to come into being, so that the *Régence* was a transitional period of the greatest significance. There were, of course, many other *ébénistes* who followed Cressent's lead, and it is always dangerous to attach too much importance to the work of one man, but his place as prime mover in the change from Classical-Baroque grandeur to Rococo lightness and grace can hardly be challenged. His position as cabinet-maker to the Regent ensured for him the authority necessary for putting his ideas into action, and they accorded well with the mood of the day. Everyone was fed to the teeth with Louis XIV's megalomania, expressed in every possible way from bullying to Boulle-work. The French were more than ready for a bit of light-hearted and light-headed nonsense.

Louis XV (1723-1774). They certainly got it, in full measure. The young Louis became king in 1723 and his uncle, Philip of Orleans, died later in the same year. Charles Cressent was still a relatively young man, and his work and that of his contemporaries now received further impetus from the slightly mad inspirations of the goldsmith and architect, Meissonier. He it was who, more than any other individual, dreamed up the manner of the Rococo or—to give it its French name—*rocaille*, meaning rock-and-shell work; though neither rocks nor shells are necessarily to be found in Rococo furniture.

The Baroque had been, originally, a restless spirit, but under the classicism of Le Brun and his school it had become, like any reformed rake, a model of rather depressing propriety. Now, its illegitimate daughter, the Rococo, pirouetted into circulation, apparently free from parental discipline and exhibiting all the waywardness once displayed by the Baroque in its youth, combined with the quaintness inherited from a Chinese mother. Louis XIV, it may be remembered, had shared the seventeenth century passion for oriental art, which is essentially grave in its concept of beauty. Given the Rococo treatment, *chinoiserie* was made as gay and amusing as everything else in the repertoire. The school of Meissonier and all its imitators, from one end of Europe to another, saw the Chinese as funny little men in comic little hats who paddled absurd little boats across laughable little lakes with ludicrous little houses on their banks and witty little waterfalls emptying themselves upstream.

This was the oriental element that, combined with asymmetrically arranged, ragged, C-shaped scrolls, and a generous allowance of rocks, shells, foliage, flowers, and bows of ribbon, went to make up the ornament of the Rococo. All these motifs, and many more besides, found their way on to the superbly made furniture of the Louis XV period. They were sometimes carved, forming part of the outline of such things as mirror-frames and wall-brackets, which were mostly gilded, but they also found a resting-place in flat and gently curving surfaces, by way of marquetry and lacquer decoration. Painting on the wood itself, or on metal panels inserted in the framework of cabinet doors, became a favourite method of embellishment as the style progressed, idyllic scenes in the '*fête galante*' manner of Watteau and his followers being popular subjects. Elaborately shaped china-cabinets with panels signed 'Martin' are not at all uncommon, but most of them that one sees are nineteenth-century copies, 'Vernis Martin' being a patent lacquer, invented by two brothers named Martin, about 1730.

Such elaboration of shape is, however, a most important feature of French Rococo. The emphasis is always on sinuous lines—indeed, it is often difficult to find a straight one in the entire composition of a piece of *Louis Quinze*. Even flat surfaces are avoided like the plague, unless they are absolutely essential to the function of the article, as in the case of a table-top.

The utmost skill was needed for such work, and the leading cabinet-makers were able to demand high prices. Some of the more successful ones made large fortunes. Their guild was powerful and entry into it was difficult. Not all the Paris *ébénistes* belonged to it, those in certain specified districts of the city being exempted from the law which compelled the rest to belong to the guild or seek employment with a master man who belonged already. Members of the guild usually signed their products by stamping their initials into the woodwork in an inconspicuous place. The makers of ormolu mounts, especially the chisellers, also sometimes signed their work—and not only the great ones such as Jacques Caffieri and his son Philippe. Some never signed their work at all.

Ormolu at its best is a form of bronze—an alloy of copper and zinc, sometimes with the addition of tin. The less zinc used in proportion to copper, the better the bronze. In the hands of artists like the Caffieri's, it was subjected to a long and complicated process of modelling, casting, chiselling, bathing in acid, burnishing and, finally, gilding with gold lacquer—the *'or moulu'*, or ground gold, that gives it its name. The epitome of French furniture collecting is reached with the acquisition of a piece signed by both cabinet-maker and bronze-maker.

If you are fortunate enough to own a good piece of French furniture, it is always worth looking over it carefully for a mark of this kind, as the commercial value is often enhanced enormously by its presence. You might even be the lucky owner of a *commode* or *bureau-plat* (not a bureau in the English sense, but a flat-topped writing-table) by the greatest of all the Louis XV cabinet-makers, J. F. Oeben, who was appointed *ébéniste du roi* in 1754. He had learned his trade from André Charles Boulle, cabinet-maker to the previous king, and in his turn taught J. H. Riesener, who was to carry on this tradition by receiving the same honour in the next reign. Oeben died before his last great work, a cylinder-top desk for Louis XV, could be finished, and it was completed by his pupil. This piece is to be seen in the Louvre, and a fellow to it, said by some to have been made for the King of Poland, is in London, in the Wallace Collection. By others, it is thought to be a nineteenth-century copy of the finest quality, and is a salutary warning to intending buyers of antique furniture to find out as much as possible about the subject in advance, and then to have a clear understanding of what is claimed by the seller for the article he is offering. It also raises the interesting question—is there a point at which the bogus becomes authentic?

Personally, I think there is. The difficulty lies in knowing just how to define it in each particular case. A Chelsea or Worcester copy of a Chinese, Meissen or Sèvres porcelain plate is, in a sense, a 'fake', but it is genuine enough, and of greater value than the original, to the collector of old English porcelain. Most, if not all, such copies were made as naïve imitations of what were then *contemporary* originals. That is not the same as reproducing, at a later date, things of a past age. Yet, even when this has clearly been the intention, there are many categories of antiques where such reproductions are accepted readily enough as authentic works of art, in their own right. The Chinese were always much given to reproducing the work of earlier periods, while in Europe, from the Renaissance onwards, interest in classical art has been revived from time to time to such effect that vast numbers of imitations, some of them downright slavish, are now old enough to be 'antiques'. It is only long familiarity with this or that department of collecting that enables one to know where to draw the line—and even then, as the years hurry by, the inevitable tendency is for that line to shift, to move forward from 1830 in Chelsea to 1860 in Kensington (see p. 14). There are purists who try to insist that a 'genuine antique' must be, not only of a certain age but also of the period which it *purports* to be. In practice, this does not work out very well, and strictly applied, it would lead to the casting out as unworthy of a great many fine and beautiful things. I have some Wedgwood library busts about a hundred-and-fifty years old, which 'purport' to be Greek bronze. Do I throw them in the ash-can? Loud cries of 'yes' from members of my family who hate the sight of them!

I have digressed a little from the matter in hand because this principle is rapidly becoming a vital one so far as French furniture is concerned, and I want to make it clear that I am not making a special exception of it. The rules of collecting, such as they are, apply to it just as firmly as—if not more so than—to any other branch of connoisseurship. For that very reason, the exceptions to the rules assume a special importance, particularly for the woman who would like one or two good pieces in her drawing-room, but who, by force of circumstance or virtue, is not in so good a position to command masculine purse strings as was La Pompadour.

Prices of the finest eighteenth-century pieces are now astronomical. The record, to date, is held by a *bureau-plat* sold by

Christie's a year or two ago for 35,000 guineas (approximately $105,000). This attractive little item had been stored in a stable not very far from my home for many years. Nobody told me. Well, it's no good shutting the stable door, etc. But I wish I'd opened it.

Exceptional though this sort of price is, it is not at all unusual for pieces of *Louis Quinze* and *Louis Seize* to bring hundreds of pounds apiece, and quite a few bring thousands. Even a generation ago, before the current fashion reached present dimensions, all but the most important pieces could be purchased in Paris very reasonably—for less money, in some cases, than it cost to make them originally, and almost invariably for less than the same shops were asking for new reproductions. But that was thirty years ago, and the ratio is now very different. Today, reproductions are still being made and are on sale all over Europe. They are nothing like as good as those made before the war, and they are more expensive than ever, but the eighteenth-century originals have now come into their own, and the modern copies are, in the main, much cheaper than the genuine article. (This is true of French furniture but not, necessarily, of modern reproductions of English pieces, which are often more costly than the real thing.)

There is, however, another basis of comparison. Fortunately, the lover of French furniture is not restricted to a choice between fearsomely expensive originals and somewhat less costly, but rather garish, modern copies. Following the defeat of Napoleon and the restoration of the French monarchy in 1815, there was a revival of interest in the eighteenth-century styles which continued throughout the nineteenth century and down to the present day. A hundred years and more ago, some really first-class copies were made. True, they lacked originality, but both material and workmanship were as good as that found in the things that inspired them. In fact, blasphemer that I am, I incline to the view that, technically speaking, the best copies made between 1840 and 1870 were superior to the medium-grade originals. In the main, they were not intended to be fakes; a reproduction becomes a fake only when the intention is to pass it off as the original. The men who made them were proud of their skill and often signed their products with their own names, as their forbears had done.

PLATE I (*above*). English Gothic Oak Chest of plank construction, sixteenth century. (*By permission of Mr. Ralph Cox, Lincoln.*) PLATE II (*right*). Italian Baroque Carved Pine Frame, seventeenth century. (*By permission of Mr. T. G. B. Brodie-Smith.*)

PLATE III (*left*). Spanish *Papilera*, mounted on a stand braced with wrought iron, seventeenth century. (*By permission of Mr. David Tron, London.*) PLATE IV (*right*). Indo-Portuguese Cabinet-of-Drawers on stand, of red-wood, seventeenth century. (*By permission of Mr. T. G. B. Brodie-Smith.*)

PLATE V (*right*). English Oak Chair with solid seat and high, panelled back, seventeenth century. (*In the author's possession.*)
PLATE VI(A) (*below left*). Welsh Oak Open Court Cupboard with 'cup-and-cover' supports, late sixteenth century. (*By permission of The National Welsh Folk Museum.*) PLATE VI(B) (*below right*). Welsh Oak *Cwpwrdd Deuddarn* (two-part Standing Cupboard), early eighteenth century. (*By permission of the National Welsh Folk Museum.*)

PLATE VII (*left*). English Walnut and Yew-wood Escritoire with drawers below and fall-front writing leaf above, early eighteenth century. (*By permission of Dr. T. L. Morris.*) PLATE VIII (*below*). English secrétaire-sideboard, veneered with olive-wood, mid-eighteenth century. Inset shows the writing leaf extended. (*In the author's possession.*)

PLATE IX. French Landscape-Marquetry Commode in natural and stained pearwood, *bois de citron* and walnut, within bandings of tulipwood and purpleheart, the windows of the houses inlaid with mother-o'-pearl. The ormolu mounts and handles in the classical style, the legs retaining the cabriole curve. Transitional period, Louis XV to Louis XVI, third quarter of the eighteenth century. (*By permission of Monsieur Nogatch, Paris.*)

PLATE X (*left*). English Elbow-Chair in Mahogany, Chippendale period, mid-eighteenth century.
PLATE XI (*below*). Dutch *bombé* commode veneered in walnut with rococo handles, mid-eighteenth century. (*In the author's possession.*)

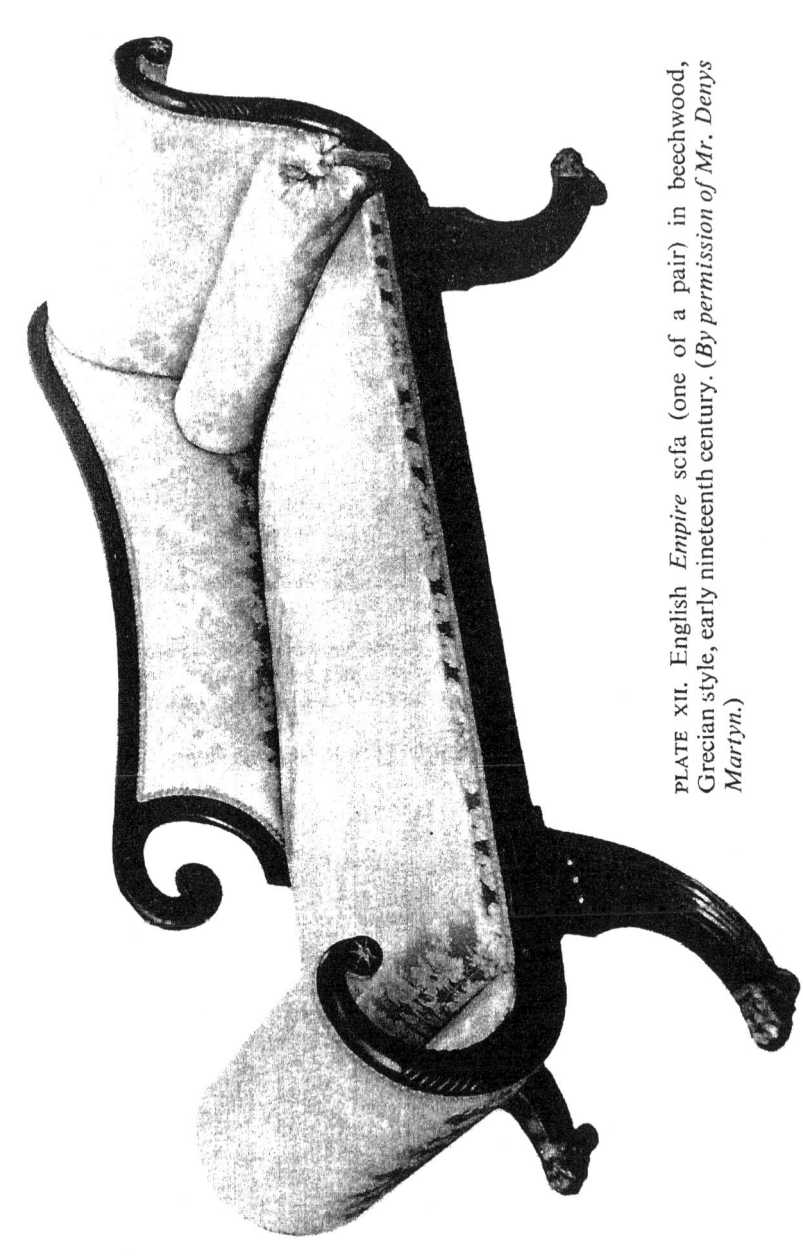

PLATE XII. English *Empire* sofa (one of a pair) in beechwood, Grecian style, early nineteenth century. (*By permission of Mr. Denys Martyn.*)

PLATE XIII (*above*). English Music-Canterbury in rosewood, inlaid with brass, of lyre shape, early nineteenth century. (*In the author's possession.*) PLATE XIV (*below*). Welsh Oak Corner-Dresser, the one side with pot-board and turned columnar legs, the other with enclosed cupboards, on bracket feet, late eighteenth or early nineteenth century. (*Formerly in the author's possession.*)

There is a great deal of this nineteenth-century work about which compares favourably enough with that of a hundred years before, at least from a furnishing point of view, and very favourably indeed with modern reproductions, from *every* point of view, including the financial one, because it is appreciably cheaper than the new and infinitely cheaper than the really old. So far as age is concerned, much of it is now 'antique', according to the more liberal interpretation of the term, and as each year goes by, so more of it passes into this category. Consequently, it is steadily appreciating in value, and good examples command respectable prices.

Of course, however fine a reproduction is, and however mellow the advance of time has made it, it is still a spurious article to the incorrigible seeker after authenticity, who will always prefer a thing to be completely of its own period, however late that period, and however humble the article. There are those who would prefer a simple Victorian kitchen chair of 1860, that doesn't try to be anything else, to a magnificent 1860 copy of a 1760 *fauteuil*. I respect this point of view, and go a long way towards sharing it, but I also sympathize with those prepared to accept the old reproduction that is so good, it needs an expert to tell the difference.

No matter to which of these schools of thought you belong, and even if, like me, you have a foot in each, the great thing, always, is to know what you are about, and to be wary of paying far too much for a reproduction in the mistaken belief that it is a genuine piece going at bargain price. That is the sad but almost inevitable fate of the inveterate bargain-hunter.

Distinguishing between the genuine *Louis Quinze* and the best nineteenth-century copies is not at all easy. The best indications are to be found in the technical methods employed rather than in style. Stylistically, the later pieces are usually fairly accurate, though it is possible to detect, very often, a certain lack of refinement in feeling, a suggestion of vulgarity and flamboyance where there should be an aristocratic elegance. This snobbish approach is not reliable, however, as the same pandering to bourgeois taste is evident in some of the mediocre work of the best periods.

Where methods and materials are concerned, we are on firmer ground, yet even here, quick-sands are there to trap us.

Mid-eighteenth-century furniture was almost entirely hand-made, and the tell-tale marks left by mechanical saws are condemnatory; but their absence is no proof of an early date of manufacture, since many of the nineteenth-century craftsmen disdained the use of machinery. Such marks can also be removed by sandpapering, or covered by veneers. Veneers themselves usually tell us a great deal. In general, old veneers are quite thick—anything up to one eighth of an inch—while those used from about 1840 onwards are relatively thin, modern ones being of paper-thickness. But old veneers may have been rubbed down in the process of re-polishing, giving them a deceptively modern appearance, or transferred from a genuine but unsaleable article to a modern carcase of attractive design. It is easy to be misled, either way, into thinking a piece is older or newer than it really is. Many good judges rightly attach great importance to the quality of the ormolu mounts on Louis XV furniture (see p. 86), which is usually of a high standard on genuine pieces, exhibiting the fine chiselling by hand of the *ciseleur*; whereas the bulk of reproductions lack this finesse, being mounted with bronzes to which little beyond gilding has been done after the casting process. This reliance on ormolu as a guide to genuineness is really rather dangerous, overlooking, as it does, the extremely high standard achieved by some of the copyists. I have also seen relatively modern pieces of good quality with eighteenth-century mounts, doubtless removed from some badly damaged original.

I am sorry if all this sounds thoroughly discouraging, but it would be foolish to pretend that there are any completely safe guides to the recognition of authentic pieces of this or any other period. Experience and the advice of people who have already gained it are the only true guides. Regular visits to the galleries that specialize in French furniture provide the best means of learning. The auction-rooms of London, Paris, and New York can also be very instructive. It should be noted that such shame-making words as 'reproduction' or 'copy' seldom appear in the sale catalogues. Where the piece is described, not simply as 'Louis XV' but 'Louis XV *style*', it is usually safe to conclude that the auctioneers do not consider it to be genuine; the italics, needless to say, are mine.

Style is, however, the first thing to master, and in addition to what I have already said about the general shapes and form of decoration on Louis XV furniture, it might be useful to add a few notes about the individual types that characterize the period (see Fig. 15).

The *commode* has already been mentioned. Usually *bombé* in shape, very often with a marble top, it may be of three-drawer depth, in which case it comes near to the ground; or it may be of two-drawer depth only, and stand on relatively high legs of elegant cabriole form. An important feature of most of the better examples is that the bottom edge of a drawer appears to meet the top edge of the one below it, without any visible dividing rail. The advantage of this arrangement was that the front of the commode could be decorated with lacquer or marquetry, and embellished with ormolu, as though it were one uninterrupted surface. As a girl I know once innocently said, 'I like the French drawers that come down in one piece.'

This leads one, only too naturally, to a recognition of the fact that a great deal of *Louis Quinze* furniture is essentially feminine in character. The king was very much under the influence of his more permanent mistresses, especially Madame de Pompadour —a woman of exquisite taste and high intelligence, whose influence on the arts of the period can hardly be exaggerated in its importance. Many ladies of fashion were not merely literate but literary by aspiration and habit, much given to letter-writing, in the same sort of way as their modern counterparts are telephone-addicts. Pieces of furniture were specially designed to meet their needs, among them being the *secrétaire* and the *bonheur-du-jour*. The former was the first to appear, at the beginning of the reign. It has a fall-front like an English bureau, but it is vertical, not sloping, when in the closed position, with a cupboard enclosed by a pair of doors below. (Somewhat similar pieces, less elaborately shaped, appeared in England during the reign of Anne.) The *bonheur-du-jour* came later, towards the middle of the century, and was so named because it really was the 'success of the day', making an instant appeal as a combined desk and toilet-table. It assumes various shapes, and great ingenuity was often lavished on fitting it out with secret drawers that leap out at the touch of a concealed spring. Essentially, it was a small writing-table with an upper stage comprising a nest of drawers or a cupboard, sometimes enclosed by 'tambour' doors. These are made by mounting narrow slats of wood on to a canvas backing, so that they will run within guides on a curve. Modern roll-top desks, not to mention sliding garage doors, work in much the same way.

The *bonheur-du-jour* probably developed from the *bureau-plat* —the flat-topped writing table—used in conjunction with the *cartonnier*, a nest of open shelves and drawers, rather like the upper part of our old friend the cabinet-on-stand, but without enclosing doors. The *cartonnier* was often most elegantly shaped, with domed top and scrolled ends. Normally it hung from the wall or rested on a side-table near the *bureau-plat*, but there are rare instances of the one being attached to the other, the whole thing conceived as one piece, as was the *bonheur-du-jour*. In its turn, the *bureau-plat* is derived from the Boulle writing-table of the Louis XIV period, and if we go back even farther, we find heavy-looking oak and solid walnut examples of the Louis XIII style (see p. 42) with a nest of drawers fitted to the top. Thus we have the interesting process, over a century or more, whereby the desk with a superstructure of drawers, in a very masculine form, first sheds them and then, ultimately, recovers them in a very feminine form. And while we are being academic, it might be worth mentioning that 'bureau' was originally the name of the cotton material used for covering the tops of desks.

Another instance of a change of meaning is the word '*bergère*'. In its native language, even, it has a fascinating range—shepherdess, nymph, morning cap, wagtail, and cushioned arm-chair. If someone asks a Frenchman if he wants to buy a *bergère*, what does he think is being offered to him? Presumably he just says 'yes', and hopes he won't get a wagtail or a morning cap. Asked the same question, an Englishman could be excused for thinking that the item on the market was an arm-chair—cushioned, certainly, but with caned back and arms, for that is what 'bergère' has meant to the furniture trade in Britain, since the late eighteenth century. Although cane was extensively used in France during the *Louis Quinze* period, the term 'bergère' does not imply the use of it. A *bergère*, in the terminology of French furniture, is an arm-chair with padded back and arms, and a cushioned seat.

In this way, it is distinct from the *fauteuil*—an elbow-chair, with open arms, padded back and seat, and no cushion. Sometimes made with a very deep seat and well-sloped back, as a reclining chair, it is a *fauteuil Voltaire*. The old boy seems to have been something of an authority on the subject, noting that 'ladies can be seen reclining on sofas and day-beds without causing embarrassment to their friends.'

The *Louis Quinze* period produced a great variety of such things. There was the *duchesse*—a day-bed formed by adding one or two extensions to a *bergère*; the *marquise*, a medium-sized sofa with open arms and padded back, and the *panier*, a type with padded back and arms flowing into a continuous curve, so that it forms, as its name suggests, a basket-shape into which the occupant can snuggle very comfortably.

Comfort combined with elegance is the keynote of Louis XV arm-chairs and sofas. One of his daughters remarked that it was only her cosy *bergère* which stopped her from entering a convent. Indulgence in a few such luxuries might well reconcile many a woman to the disappointments and disillusionment of modern life.

There are many more things to choose from, besides the types described above, but some of them are more typical of the next period—the Neo-Classic style of Louis XVI (see p. 115 *et seq.*).

Most styles are continuous, flowing into and overlapping each other, and these are no exception. There was a reaction against the Rococo before the end of Louis XV's reign, and a transitional style had in fact developed as early as what might be called the Pompadour period. It became well established during the years when Madame du Barry was the king's favourite. The process is marked by a gradual return to straight lines and formal decoration. Characteristically transitional pieces retain the flowing line of the cabriole leg, but employ classical motifs for the ormolu mounts. (See Plate IX.)

Such subtleties mostly find expression in the city-made furniture. On p. 48, attention was drawn to the pleasing character of so many of the country-made pieces, and this applies particularly to the *Louis Quinze* style, which continued, so far as they are concerned, with little change, until well into the nineteenth century. I think this continuing popularity may be explained by the fact that the modified Rococo designs of the country craftsmen were essentially more suited to their technical skills than were the Neo-Classic styles, and they had the good sense to go on doing what they could do well, long after their colleagues in the capital had abandoned the Rococo.

As for the rest of Europe, the influence of France was, at mid-century, paramount over the greater part of the Continent. French was the language of diplomacy, and all educated people learned to speak and write it. Many Englishmen, even, were tolerably good at it. Everything in the way of architecture, sculpture, painting, and furniture that appeared at Versailles and in Paris was assiduously copied, or at least emulated, in Berlin, Vienna and St Petersburg. Then—as now—the women of Europe eagerly awaited news of the latest Paris fashions.

National traditions affected design to a greater or lesser extent, peasant pieces retaining their local flavour in all countries, and city-made articles responding very readily to Gallic influence.

Italy

Meissonier himself, 'creator' of the Rococo, was Italian, and Italian versions of *'Louis Quinze'* may be recognized by the extreme forms which the *bombé* curve was wont to take, the extent of the protrusion often being grotesquely out of proportion to the size of the piece. Small commodes with only two drawers, and consequently rather high in the leg, can fit well into the recesses of modern flats, the depth of the recess distracting from the obesity of the piece. These sometimes turn up in pairs and are best used symmetrically, with tall and fairly plain pier-glasses above them to give them much-needed height and dignity.

Some very gay furniture was made in Venice at this period, the entire surface being painted with a ground-colour of pale yellow, apple green or bright blue, with Chinese or floral motifs scattered over it. As the line was sinuous and the surface undulating, the effect is sometimes rather hectic, and the odd-looking settees, chairs, chests-of-drawers, beds, and desks that resulted need placing with great care if the result is not to look like a Venetian carnival. (Of course, you may *want* it to look like that; in which case, the best of Venetian luck to you.) Such pieces have, in the past, been bought very reasonably in English country house sales, and even in London auction-rooms, but the prices have advanced since Italian dealers have been buying up, systematically, the things that left their country many years ago.

Spain

There is some very interesting Spanish Rococo furniture—in

particular, a class that includes commodes, bow-fronted corner cupboards and side-tables, decorated with bone marquetry inlaid into veneers of olive-wood. These pieces are usually described as German, but at least some of them were made in Majorca, and are still to be seen in the palaces of the aristocracy in Palma and in the country houses, the names of which are prefixed by the word 'son', which were used as hunting lodges. The marquetry often illustrates hunting scenes. The *bombé* line is exploited discreetly, in contrast to the usual Italian exuberance described above. Palma has been a great sea-port for centuries, which probably accounts for the amount of this furniture that has found its way to other parts of the world. It has a flavour of its own that may not be to everyone's taste, as the hunting scenes often have a savage quality. Strongly recommended as a presentation piece to a retiring M.F.H.

The *bombé* swell is more pronounced in Rococo furniture of the Spanish mainland, but otherwise the style is often rendered with restraint, and an affinity with English forms of the Queen Anne and early Georgian period is particularly noticeable in the fashioning of chair-drames.

Spanish countrified furniture tends to be more conscious of the Rococo influence than was usual elsewhere outside France, and again it is the chair which demonstrates this most clearly. I have seen some very pleasing examples, attractively small in size and highly suitable for use in the smaller kind of home, with solid seats, cabriole legs joined by under-framing, and backs composed of interlaced curves. They are usually of solid walnut, strongly constructed and very heavy for their size.

Germany and Sweden

The Teutonic and Scandinavian peoples seem to have retained a strong element of the Baroque in their handling of the Rococo, going so far as to apply the twist principle to the new line, so that frame settees appear with double cabriole legs that coil around each other most alarmingly. The hooped frames of chair-backs also double up, with complex carving and fretting between inner and outer frame. An otherwise English-looking chair-back splat was often interpreted with so literal an adherence to the asymmetry of the Rococo that it presents two different profiles. This is not to say that extremely good work was not done in Germany:

on the contrary, some of the leading Paris *ébénistes* were of German origin. More will be said of them in the next chapter, and of their achievement in the reign of Louis XVI.

The Netherlands

Retracing our steps to the end of the seventeenth century, when William of Orange was also King of England, we find, not unnaturally, that many of the forms which furniture took were common not only to these two countries, but also to the American Colonies; but national characteristics very soon asserted themselves, and from the early eighteenth century onwards, the distinctions become fairly clear. The Dutch preference for bold floral marquetry persisted for another hundred years, the importance of flowers to the life and economy of Holland being, perhaps, a conditioning factor. In England, marquetry, as a rule was employed with restraint. In America, it was used hardly at all at this time, although inlaying into the solid, instead of into a veneered ground as in the case of marquetry, was not unusual. The Dutch influence is very marked in much early eighteenth-century American furniture having this kind of decoration, the tulip—for which many an early settler from Holland must have retained a nostalgic affection—being a common device.

Another feature which helps to differentiate Dutch work from English is thicker turning than was customary in Britain. The British have had, from the sixteenth century onwards, a great fondness for wood-turning, and in the early 1700's, they seem to have delighted in reducing the narrow sections to the very minimum, with results not always wholly consistent with practicability. The stretchers which comprise the underframing of Queen Anne chairs have sometimes been fined down to such a degree of slimness on the lathe that they have been unable to withstand the many years of hard wear without snapping. The Dutch employed either thicker turnings, or a flattish, shaped stretcher that was never allowed within reach of a lathe.

As the century progressed, and the sinuous lines of the Rococo wove their way from France across Europe, the Dutch craftsmen adopted the *bombé* shape with enthusiasm but a certain lack of delicacy. Often they used its swelling line for the front only of chests-of-drawers, bureaux and bureau-bookcases, leaving the ends flat. A link between front and end is provided with a broadly canted corner, to which heavily carved paw-feet, in place of French ormolu ones, are affixed. The Dutch version of the *bombé* is often quite distinct from the French in that the swell is lower down the carcase-line, so that the upper half is almost vertical. In the description of the *bombé* form on p. 83, I mentioned that I have heard it termed 'pregnant'; to pursue this figure of speech a little further, the Dutch version is rather that of a pregnancy being carried rather low.

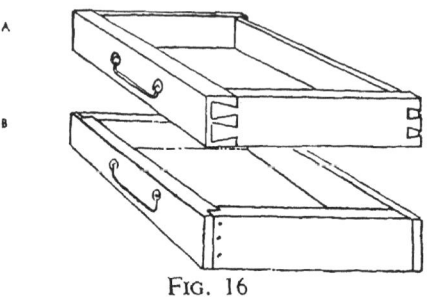

FIG. 16
Methods of Drawer-construction
A. Dovetail joint: the usual English method.
B. Shouldering: more common on continental furniture.

For a few years either way of 1700, there was an Anglo-Dutch class of furniture, some of which defies final analysis. It could have been made in Holland and brought to Britain; it could have been made in Britain by Dutch immigrant craftsmen; or it could have been made by Englishmen closely imitating Dutch models and methods. A useful, but not infallible, indication is the method of jointing the fronts of drawers to the sides. Dutch and German craftsmen often employed what is termed 'shouldering', while the English favoured dove-tailing. (The difference is better explained visually—see Fig. 16.) However, there was a great deal of coming and going and exchanging of ideas, and such points as these must be taken together with the rest of the evidence when inquests are being held. They are the sort of considerations that the modern home-maker, only interested in how the end-product is going to look in the living area of his open-plan maisonette, regards as a crashing bore. But once he gets started on the subject, he will finish up, like the rest of us, contemplating his early eighteenth-century chair with the very

Dutch-looking marquetry in the splat, and the equally English-looking turning of the stretchers, and caring quite passionately whether it started life in Haarlem or Highgate; and he won't be much the wiser for reading this, I'm afraid.

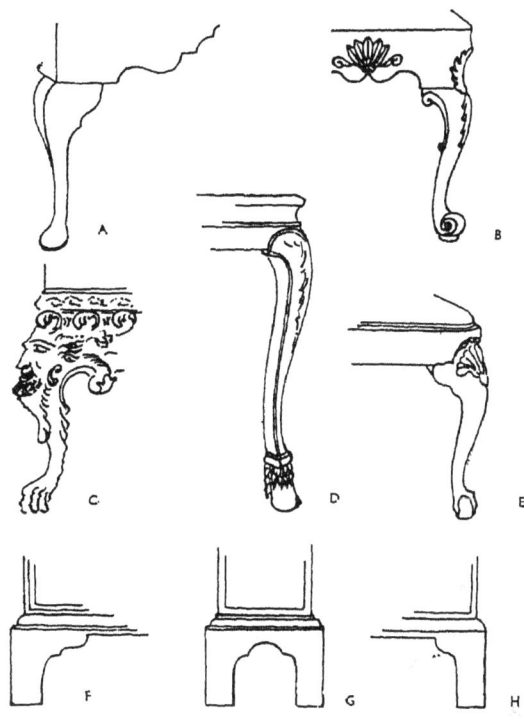

Fig. 17
Queen Anne and Early Georgian Periods
Legs and Feet on early-eighteenth century English Furniture
A. Simple cabriole leg with pad foot.
B. Cabriole leg showing French influence, with scrolled or 'whorled' foot.
C. Elaborately carved leg showing Italian and German influence, with satyr mask on the knee, and paw foot.
D. Elegant form of cabriole leg with pony foot.
E. Characteristic early Georgian form, with shell carved on knee and claw-and-ball foot.
  G and H are variations of the bracket foot, in use throughout the eighteenth century.

Britain

If the chair in question, be it English, Dutch, or anything else, has cabriole legs united by stretchers, it almost certainly belongs to the first twenty years or so of the eighteenth century—unless, of course, it is a downright modern copy. Because its shape necessitates cutting across the grain to some extent, the cabriole leg was at first distrusted by many practical woodworkers. It was, after all, a logical development of the scroll-leg, which had always been provided with underframing, and it was perfectly natural to employ similar precautions with the new, elegant line that first appeared in a pure form about 1700. The more conservative craftsmen continued to use underframing with the cabriole for another twenty years, but adventurous spirits began to discard such clumsy devices early in Anne's reign, allowing the cabriole-legged chair to stand on its own feet, unaided.

Anne (1702-1714). The feet themselves take varying forms (Fig. 17). The commonest is a simple pad. To my taste, it is also the pleasantest. More rarely, we find an English piece of this period with a scroll-foot—either a downward, backward-curving scroll or an upward, forward, curving variety, which sometimes has a peg-like stilt below it, raising it an inch or two above floor-level. Other favourites were carved to represent the feet of animals, a lion's paw or a pony's hoof. This was more or less consistent with the shape of the cabriole leg itself, which really owed its derivation to the use, in classical antiquity, of the goat's leg as a decorative motif. (The recurrence of this form, in its Pan- and other satyr-associations, is an interesting one from which anthropologists with a Freudian turn of mind might well deduce a colourful explanation.) The ball-and-claw foot was also a revival of a very early type. Known to the Ancient Egyptians and Chinese, it first made its appearance on English furniture in the early years of the eighteenth century, and has remained a firm favourite with the manufacturers of dining-room suites down to the present day. It is now so familiar that its rather grotesque and frightening implications do not register with most people, but, Freud apart, I can never look at a well-carved claw-and-ball foot without wincing. I see myself as the ball, and the Tax Collector as the claw. This is not quite the significance intended by the old mythologies, in which the ball symbolized the orb of power, temporal and spiritual, held in the grip of authority. I have often noticed that people with a particular liking for this type of foot also have a liking for power.

The wood-carver exercised great skill on the carving of feet. Often it was his only chance to show his paces, as carving was well-disciplined during the Queen Anne period, seldom being allowed to dominate a piece but used only to provide points of focal interest, such as a shell as the knee-cap of a cabriole leg, or a neat, unobtrusive scroll where the vase-shaped centre-splat of a chair back unites with the swan-necked frame. The emphasis as this time was on elegance of line, strength of construction, good proportions and the fine finish provided by carefully veneered surfaces. Graciousness was supplanting grandiloquence, and masculine solemnity of the Baroque was slowly softening in preparation for the feminine frivolity of the Rococo.

This process began, if anything, earlier in Britain than in France. The English had not been under the dictatorship of Louis XIV, and in moving away from the more ponderous style of the late seventeenth century, the extravagant gestures of the rebel were not necessary to them. The process was gradual—evolution rather than revolution. As a consequence—and perhaps because of a slight check administered with the coming of the House of Hanover in 1714 and the adoption of certain heavier, Germanic forms—English furniture never really tried to be as amusing as did the French work we have considered in this chapter.

Although it is not, at the moment of writing, the most fashionable period, fine-quality pieces of Queen Anne walnut yet command fairly high prices—sometimes very high indeed. This applies especially to the smaller and rarer pieces, such as little bureaux raised on cabriole legs, and 'bachelor' chests-of-drawers with tops of double thickness hinged on the front edge so that they can be extended to rest on sliding supports (technically known as lopers). (See Fig. 18.)

Of the larger pieces, some are considered 'important', e.g. bureau-bookcases in red lacquer. One or two outstanding specimens have been known to bring as much as 5,000 guineas ($15,000) apiece during recent years. Some of the bigger types, however, can be bought at reasonable prices, and the idea that they are out of place in the modern home is fallacious. The double chest-of-drawers, or 'chest-on-chest', which first appeared

Fig. 18

English Furniture, first half of the eighteenth century
A. Chest-on-chest.
B. Mirror in decorated frame with swan-neck pediment.
C. Bachelor chest-of-drawers with top extending forward.
D. Wing arm-chair.
E. Standard-chair, the back with solid centre-splat, shaped seat and cabriole legs.
F. Oval flap-table on cabriole legs.
G. Brass loop-handle and contemporary lock-plate.

in Britain about 1710, is a good case in point. Many dealers find them difficult to sell—even the fine, early examples with beautifully figured walnut veneers—but, in fact, they are great space-savers, occupying no more floor space than would a substantial chest-of-drawers, and providing double the accommodation. Later examples of mahogany, and oak ones of all periods, are in even less demand, although there is considerable interest, in America, in the highboy or chest-on-stand, which actually wastes space, the lower stage consisting mainly of legs which, as often as not, are barely strong enough to support the heavy carcase above. What the poor old chest-on-chest has done to deserve such comparative neglect, I really don't know.

I would, however, offer a word of warning about Queen Anne walnut and, indeed, all veneered furniture. It is broadly true that the finest furniture is veneered, but it can suffer badly from the effects of excessive central heating. In humid heat, veneers lift, because they were originally fixed with animal glue, not the synthetic kind that science has been obliged to perfect in order to combat the destructive properties of the steam-pipes. Often there is unequal expansion and contraction of veneer and solid foundation. Even pieces constructed entirely of solid timber, without any delicate surface of veneer, deeply resent being placed too near a piping hot radiator, and register their protest by splitting—sometimes very noisily, with a crack like a pistol-shot.

Providing you can arrange your life so that the heating arrangements do not engender a tropical temperature, the following types of early eighteenth-century furniture are strongly to be recommended.

During this period, the fashion of dining in small groups, begun in Restoration times, persisted. Although oak gateleg tables continued to be made, they were largely replaced by 'flap' tables, oval or circular when erected, and constructed in solid walnut. These tables have four cabriole legs, two of which are hinged to support the flaps. They fold down to a conveniently small size, and when extended are more comfortable to sit at than the gateleg, having no underframing to get in the way (Fig. 18).

Queen Anne dining chairs, handsome though they are, are less easy to use in a small room, the generous width of the seats, and the extra projection of the cabriole legs, demanding a certain spaciousness. For those who can accommodate them, there is much pleasure to be had from their flowing lines and the beautiful golden brown to which old walnut mellows. A characteristic shape is illustrated in Fig. 18, the outstanding features being the rounded cresting rail and seat, blending happily with the well-shaped leg, and the vase-shaped splat of the back, subtly curved to fit the human spine.

One of the attractions of antique furniture is the versatility of many of the pieces, and this is especially true of the Queen Anne writing- or dressing-table. It takes two forms, the first

FIG. 19

Basic shapes for English Furniture, early- to mid-eighteenth century

A. Kneehole writing- or dressing-table on cabriole legs.
B. Simple chest-of-drawers.
C. Chest-on-stand ('tallboy' or 'highboy') composed of table (A) used as a stand for chest (B).
D. Kneehole desk or dressing-table on bracket feet, with recessed cupboard; essentially a variation of the chest-of-drawers (B).

comprising a table-top with three drawers below—a shallow one at the centre flanked by two deeper ones—mounted on cabriole legs. If you take a good look at Fig. 19, you will see how this type of thing forms the stand of a tallboy, and also of a bureau. In the same way, a chest-of-drawers, mounted in various ways, takes on a variety of appearances. Furniture of this period was essentially simple in conception, relying on the permutations possible with a few basic shapes to produce a wide range of articles.

The second type of writing-table is really a chest-of-drawers with a kneehole provided. So as not to waste valuable space, a small cupboard is recessed in the kneehole (Fig. 19).

These chest-forms were supported on 'bracket' feet, which began to replace the 'bun' type of the William and Mary period at the beginning of the eighteenth century. They are extremely practical for holding heavy pieces a few inches off the floor, and are fairly easy to replace when necessary. This necessity does, inevitably, arise, and carefully replaced bracket feet are not, regarded as seriously depreciating the value of any but the rarest and most important pieces. (Fig. 17, F, G & H.)

These are the articles of outstandingly fine quality and beauty of design, prized by 'advanced' collectors, for whom this book does not pretend to cater, but such pieces provide a basis of comparison when we come down to earth and choose things of the same period, within our own price-range, and the opportunity to examine them, in shop or sale-room, private house or public museum, should never be missed. They are what remain to us of the output of the great craftsmen of that time, some of whom are known to us by name, but little of whose work can be identified.

There is comparatively little English furniture of any period that can be safely attributed to this or that maker. The custom of signing pieces—usual and, to some extent, obligatory in France—never took hold in Britain. Country craftsmen sometimes carved initials on chests and cupboards, but these were more often those of the owner rather than the maker of the piece. Very few London makers appended any kind of signature or trademark of a permanent nature to their work. From the late seventeenth century onwards, many of them stuck paper trade-labels on the backs of pieces, and on drawer-bottoms, but relatively few of them have remained attached to the articles. Sir

Ambrose Heal made a remarkable collection of these labels; an exhaustive study of them, and of pieces bearing them, was made a few years ago by Mr Ralph Edwards and Miss Margaret Jourdain, who published their findings in a work of the greatest interest and value to the keen student.[1] Great gaps still exist in the knowledge available, however. On the one hand, there is a great deal of anonymous work, and on the other, a list of craftsmen about whom little is known, in many cases, beyond their names and addresses. Relating the one to the other is not by any means easy, but it is possible, in a number of instances, to make reasonably safe attributions, supported by documentary evidence of one kind or another—labels, receipts, account-books, published designs and so on. Pieces of good quality that can be assigned in this way to a particular maker are sought after and usually sell at very much higher prices than do anonymous pieces of otherwise equal merit.

Not very long ago, I fondly imagined I had 'discovered' a piece in the bedroom of a Gloucestershire mansion, where there was to be an auction-sale. It was a bureau decorated in a curious manner supposed to be peculiar to Coxed and Woster, London cabinet-makers of the Queen Anne period, who specialized in the use of mulberry-wood veneers, inlaid with pewter stringing. Recognizing their style, I was almost sorry to find their trade-label stuck to the bottom of a drawer. There was now no chance of the thing being overlooked. Knowing I was thus in no position to buy it against competition from the big dealers, and thinking the piece of sufficient importance to merit a place in the national collection, I reported it, through a friend, to a retired official of the Victoria and Albert Museum. Much to the deflation of my ego, I was brusquely informed that my 'discovery' was well known to the powers-that-be, the ex-official himself having 'discovered' it some years before, and that the museum already had as much work by these makers as it could comfortably accommodate. I lamely left a bid of three hundred pounds, which was all I could afford to gamble, and was not surprised to learn the little bureau was subsequently 'knocked down' for three times that amount. As a consolation prize, I got a perfectly genuine marquetry chest-of-drawers, admittedly not so fine and bearing no fancy labels, but of the same period and in its way

[1] 'Georgian Cabinet Makers' (*Country Life*, 1944).

just as pleasing—for twenty-five pounds. That is the sort of difference that exists between the important and the unimportant.

George I (1714-1727). What is important to us, in attempting to grasp the fundamentals of the subject, is that while English furniture prior to 1700 is largely anonymous, with only one or two names like Grinling Gibbons and Daniel Marot to bandy about somewhat irrelevantly, from this time onwards it does become possible to describe many pieces according to the styles of individual craftsmen and designers. Unfortunately, it also becomes inevitable that these names should often be misapplied and misunderstood. One of the reasons for reading—and, indeed, for writing—a book like this is to reduce the incidence of such misapprehensions. The principle is that these names are used to describe pieces made in the manner we associate with this or that individual, not necessarily by him but by his contemporaries. A reproduction is also 'in the manner of', and care should be exercised in finding out exactly what is meant in each particular case. A 'Chippendale' chair, for example, might be a chair made by Chippendale, by another eighteenth-century maker, working to a Chippendale design, or a copy, faithful or otherwise, executed at any time during the last couple of hundred years. The use of these names is convenient. Sometimes it is just a little too convenient.

Many of the names exploited, legitimately or otherwise, are those of designers who never actually made furniture themselves. The first notable English architect to treat furniture-design as a serious part of his work was William Kent, whose inspiration largely derived from the grand Italian manner of Palladio. Kent's furniture was essentially architectural in conception, each piece being expressly intended to occupy a given position in a specific house. Some of his bookcases are of splendid proportions —veritable buildings in themselves—while his console tables, supported by carved caryatids—figures half-human, half-animal or architectural device—are magnificent if un-English in appearance. Much work of this kind was in carved *gesso*—a very hard plaster coating over a wood foundation—richly gilded. Such things were produced under Kent's direction, in the early Georgian period, for the statelier homes of England, and it is seldom that they settle down very happily in humbler surroundings. His designs are chiefly interesting as examples of the tremendous dignity to which the erstwhile restless and tormented Baroque manner could aspire under strict architectural discipline of the kind exerted by Palladio in Italy, Le Brun in France, Inigo Jones, Christopher Wren, and William Kent himself in Britain.

Quite distinct, in most ways, from this purely luxury-class was the usual run of early Georgian furniture, which carried on the best traditions of the short but important Queen Anne period, with the emphasis on good proportion, elegant lines to legs with the cabriole as the most usual shape, and rectilinear carcases. English craftsmen were slow to respond to the *Régence* influence, the *bombé* shape being little used in Britain, and at a later date, during the reign of George III. The nearest thing to it, at this time, was the so-called 'block front' which occurs, though rarely, in chests-of-drawers and bureau-bookcases. Here, the shaping is semi-serpentine but on the latitudinal plane only (see Fig. 21D). Examples of this shape occur in German and American furniture of the mid-eighteenth century, and authentic American examples are, very properly, highly prized. Some of them were doubtless shipped out from Europe, but American makers of importance were, by the beginning of the Georgian period, producing furniture every bit as good as European. (See p. 114.)

America was exporting to Britain some of the walnut which, during the reign of George I, remained the fashionable timber. The demand for it was such that there was not enough home-grown walnut to meet it, and supplies from the Continent gave out when a disease destroyed thousands of trees. Both 'black' and 'red' walnut from Virginia helped to make good the shortage, until a 'new' wood, first used about 1715 in Britain, became so popular that by the accession of George II in 1727, it had ousted walnut from favour. This latest novelty was an importation from Spanish possessions in the Caribbean, and was known as 'Spanish' mahogany.

George II (1727-1760). Early examples of mahogany furniture follow, basically, the designs employed over the previous quarter-century for walnut pieces, but certain modifications were immediately found to be necessary, since mahogany proved, at first, a difficult wood to work. These practical considerations, as much as changes in taste, accounted for some of the features of early to mid eighteenth-century work.

Although mahogany eventually came to be used, like walnut, in the form of veneers, most of the earlier work was executed in the solid, with a revival of interest in carving. Once the carvers had learned to temper their tools to suit the brittle quality of the wood, it proved a material reasonably well suited to sculpting the delicate scrolls and ribbon-work of the Rococo. Softer woods, such as pine, were used for the more fanciful mirror-frames and wall-brackets in the French manner, which were nearly always gilded, and beech was commonly employed for the frames of chairs and settees that were given this kind of finish.

Neither marquetry nor ormolu mounting were extensively used by the English at this period, and with a few important exceptions, the delicate extravagances of Louis XV *ébénistes* were avoided, in practice, by the London makers—though some of the designs which appeared were fantastic indeed. Many of them were never executed, so far as we know, in wood.

The most celebrated of the London design-books was Thomas Chippendale's *Gentleman and Cabinet Maker's Director*, the first edition of which was published in 1754, earning for its author an undying and, some think, undeserved fame. There is evidence that many of the designs were really the work of Lock and Copeland, who had published a Rococo pattern-book, under their own names, a few years earlier. But legend dies hard, and no matter what pedantic objections be raised, the bulk of mid-eighteenth-century English furniture always has been, and presumably always will be, loosely described as Chippendale. (Just how loosely is a matter I have already mentioned on p. 106). None of this proves Chippendale to be a charlatan. On the contrary, what we know of Chippendale's actual work suggests that he was a better cabinet-maker than the design-book suggests.

There are, for example, several *bombé* commodes in existence which can be attributed to him, decorated with the finest marquetry and rivalling the French cabinet-makers at their own game. These are among the important exceptions, previously mentioned, to the rule that most English work steers clear of this type of thing.

Exceptions, however, they remain, and though we are considering it, chronologically, under the general heading 'Baroque to Rococo', the bulk of mid-eighteenth century, medium-grade English furniture owes little to either of these continental styles, being either severely plain or relieved only very discreetly by a well-carved shell, a fretted ribbon or a fanciful brass handle. To this admirable class we will presently return, turning aside, for the moment, to consider English Rococo and also two styles that ran parallel with it—the so-called 'Chinese Chippendale' and 'Chippendale Gothic'. It should be borne in mind that, while

FIG. 20

English Rococo

A. Design for a 'claw table', after Ince and Mayhew, 1762.
B. Design for a chair, after Thomas Chippendale, 1754.
C. Design for a chair in Chippendale's manner, combining Gothic, Chinese and Rococo motifs, circa 1760.

all these styles originated in mid-century, during the reign of George II, they continued to be employed well into the next reign.

In their treatment of mirror-frames, overmantels and wall brackets, the English thoroughly enjoyed themselves with Rococo ornament. This is very obvious in a design-book published in 1762 by Ince and Mayhew, who were, to some extent, imitators of Chippendale. They were evidently determined to compete with the French on their own ground, as the text of the book is printed in both languages. I have attempted to reproduce one of their designs in Fig. 20A. This is one of three, described by them as 'Three very neat designs for Claw-Tables', and on the other side of the page, '*Trois Desseins élégans de Tables-à-un-seul-pied*'. I do not quite-see, myself, why a three-footed table should be shown balancing impossibly on two and be described, in French, as having only one. Tripod tables were made in large quantities at this time, in all grades, as it was the fashion to throw tea-parties for as many as a couple of hundred guests. I have read that, to meet such social demands, as many as fifty of these tables were regarded as part of the normal furnishing of a London house, but I must say I find it difficult to believe. Chippendale omits them entirely from the *Director*.

To what extent they succeeded, we do not know, but Messrs Ince and Mayhew make it clear that they hoped to do a two-way traffic, importing French furniture and exporting English.

To prove that the British could out-rock the Rococo if they really wanted to, Robert Manwaring produced, three years later, in 1765, some designs for 'rural' chairs which employ the asymmetrical shapes of tree-branches for the frames. Quite mad.

If we consider the designs published under Chippendale's name, we find ourselves rather nearer to reality. A great many pieces survive which bear a fairly strong resemblance to these engravings, but this cannot be accepted as evidence that they are his work, or that of his employees (he is supposed to have employed about twenty-two craftsmen), since his book was intended for, and was bought by, his colleagues in the trade. Anyone able to scrape together the requisite forty-eight shillings could buy a copy, and use it as a pattern-book, making modifications to suit himself. Two pounds eight shillings—about seven dollars—was a lot of money two hundred years ago; indeed, in these days of paper-backs and masses of free trade-catalogues, it still seems a high price for a book which was undoubtedly meant, at least in part, to advertise Chippendale's business. The fact that it ran into three editions suggests that the boys thought it pretty good value.

Figure 20B is taken from a design in the 1754 edition. It is typical of a great variety of mid-eighteenth-century chairs in the Rococo manner, the back having a 'camel' hump and delicately pierced splat. Chair-backs were often much more elaborate, as in the case of ribbon—or as they were then called, 'ribband'—backed specimens. The leg here is an elegant, very French version of the cabriole, terminating in a neat, upward-curling scroll. Various kinds of foot are found on chairs of the period, the claw-and-ball being met with frequently.

Reproductions of Chippendale's Rococo style are legion. Some of them are now a respectable age, and of excellent quality. Some of the ribbon-back chairs made about 1880 are good enough to command prices in the region of $450 to $600 for a set of six side-chairs and two elbow-chairs.

Frame settees—i.e. those with upholstery on the seat only—follow chair-design exactly, being built on the usual eighteenth-century principle of linking two, three or four chair-backs together.

Both Chippendale's book and that of Ince and Mayhew illustrate pieces of the kind known as 'Chinese Chippendale', and the latter even suggest 'japanning' as the most suitable finish for some. In the main, however, the *chinoiseries* of this period were not lacquered, as they had been in earlier times, but relied on shape, together with fretted and carved ornament, to achieve their rather strange purpose. Few *trained* observers had ever visited China, and no authentic report appeared until 1757 —three years after the publication of the first edition of the *Director*—when Sir William Chambers, architect to George III a few years later, and the first English member of his profession to visit the country, brought out his Designs for *Chinese Buildings, Furniture, Dresses, Etc.* He was not, personally, in sympathy with the craze for pseudo-oriental styles, and intended his book to be a corrective measure against the more fantastic conceptions of the East that were prevalent. When Chippendale produced his designs for furniture 'in the Chinese taste', he did not have the benefit of Chambers' book, or any other reliable information, to work on. Ince and Mayhew presumably had the advantage of studying the work of Chambers before getting out the drawings for their *Universal System of Household Furniture*, but their ideas seem much more in keeping with the popular conception than with the authentic report.

When Thomas Chippendale, Yorkshireman, set himself to please fashionable fancy for exotic styles, the results were curious—sometimes charming, sometimes hideous. Chairs in this oriental manner usually had square-framed backs set with geometric frets, and straight, square legs carved to match. Torchère stands for candelabra and small tables with carefully fretted galleries are among the more attractive examples of 'Chinese Chippendale' which can take their place in the small house. Some remarkable cabinets and wall-shelves, with pagoda-shaped tops, still serve admirably the purpose for which they were intended—the display of porcelain. Some very good, small examples are to be had, but they tend to be expensive. Large versions of the cabinets are to be found in the 'break-front' form: a centre section projecting a couple of inches beyond the side-pieces flanking it. This was a characteristic, and very pleasing, method of constructing bookcases and cabinets at that period. The 'Chinese Chippendale' interpretation, however, is sometimes rather much to bear. Each of the three sections has its pagoda-top, from which temple-bells of carved mahogany hang, and in place of the cupboard-section below, which break-front bookcases usually have, there is a stand of square legs that always seems to me too frail for the carcase above. Several that I have seen, based on designs in *The Universal System*, appear to have been made at a rather later date, probably during the period of revived interest in *chinoiserie* that came in the Regency, about 1815.

Even in its heyday, during the 1750's and 60's, not everyone accepted the Rococo and its oriental off-shoot. Horace Walpole heartily disapproved, preferring the odd, peculiarly English, revival of the Gothic style, so long despised (see p. 22). Fellow enthusiasts built houses complete with towers, spires, battlements, pointed arches, gargoyles and tracery, and some even went so far as to construct 'ruins' and romantic grottos in their landscaped gardens. It was, in fact, the beginning of the Romantic movement, which lasted until the late nineteenth century. Its later phases will be discussed in Chapter Six.

This first outbreak, in the middle of the eighteenth century, was catered for by the furniture-makers, and the resulting products are known as '*Chippendale Gothic*'. There was no attempt to reproduce early oak pieces. Most of the furniture in this manner was constructed of mahogany, and followed the usual shapes of the time, employing cusped arches and other Gothic ornament where, in other models, Rococo or Chinese motifs would have appeared. Indeed, so closely do all these styles run together that it is not at all unusual to find them overlapping, with pointed arches, C-scrolls and oriental lattice-work mixed up together in the same piece. Odd and alarming though this must sound, the result is often very pleasing. (See Fig. 20c.)

Like the 'Chinese Chippendale', the legs of 'Chippendale Gothic' furniture are vertical, often formed by a cluster of four columns, and represent an important break-away from the cabriole—the curving line of the Rococo which Hogarth regarded as the first essential to beauty. It is significant, too, that both these fanciful styles draw their inspiration from architecture, and though Gothic arch and Chinese pagoda may seem a far remove from Greek frieze, they are symptomatic of a paradoxical desire to discard the frills of the Rococo in favour of a more architectural style, without submitting completely to classical discipline. It was a mood that was basically affecting French as well as English design, and before proceeding with the effect on British furniture, it would be as well to look across the Channel once more. But first, we must look across the ocean, to observe the manifestations of the Rococo movement in America.

America (*Colonial Period*)

From about 1700 onwards, an ever-increasing consciousness of the need for comfort and beauty influenced the furnishing of the more well-to-do American home. As in Europe, the humbler folk continued to make or have made for them simple pieces of solid joinery, but those who could afford to do so set out to emulate London fashions. The cabriole leg arrived rather late, turned types being general until about 1720, but from then on, the cabriole remained a firm favourite for some seventy years.

English influence was dominant, many homes being furnished

very largely with pieces ordered in London. This is especially true of the planters' houses in the South. Elsewhere, a native tradition developed, and as I remarked earlier, some of the work was of the highest order, and possessed a flavour of its own. Block-fronted chests, bureaux and bureau-bookcases, mentioned on p. 107, were the speciality of John Goddard of Newport, Rhode Island, who was fond of decorating such pieces with the shell motif carved on an unusually large scale. Another important centre was Philadelphia, where William Savery, Thomas Affleck and Benjamin Randolph all produced furniture of outstanding quality. Savery worked during the second quarter of the eighteenth century, making well-shaped pieces in the Queen Anne and Early Georgian manner. Affleck and Randolph, during the third quarter, worked in Chippendale's Rococo manner, and both seem to have been devoted to the claw-and-ball foot. New York, Boston and the Connecticut Valley can all boast a respectable history of cabinet-making dating from this period.

Printed in Great Britain
by Amazon